T0392315

The Wisdom to Create Wealth and the Basic Principles of Finance in this Innovative Era

To order additional copies of this book, contact:
Xlibris
1-888-795-4274
www.Xlibris.com
Orders@Xlibris.com

ISBN: Softcover   978-1-7960-5999-1
         EBook   978-1-7960-5998-4

Library of Congress Control Number: 2019914325

Print information available on the last page

Rev. date: 09/25/2019

The Wisdom to Create Wealth and the Basic Principles of Finance in this Innovative Era

For: Kids and Adults

Gloria Ifeanyi

Dedication

I dedicate this book, **The Wisdom to Create Wealth and the Basic Principles of Finance in this Innovative Era, for: Kids and Adults.** To all the kids who want a greater future, and to adults who want financial freedom, and want to create immense wealth in this ever-changing world.

Table of Contents

Acknowledgements

I want to thank the Almighty God for making this book a success, my husband Michael for his love and support, and my kids for bringing their crafts and passion to this book.

Also, I want to thank the staff of Xlibris publishing company for their assistance in putting this book together.

Furthermore, I want to thank the members of Author Learning Center (ALC), for their motivational speech, and their assistance on the information about book writing, advertising, marketing, etc.

Lastly, I want to thank the National Society of Leadership and Success (NSLS), for the Motivational Mondays' weekly speech about leadership for NSLS members; offering enriching advice, and inspiration to start off the week.

Introduction

This personal finance book is written for kids and adults. It is for kids who want a greater future, setting their minds to gain the basic understanding of finance, acquiring the knowledge of saving money; and knowing the importance of it, for a greater tomorrow. It will also assist parents and guardians who want to set their children on the right financial part, to educate their kids in a better way.

Also, it is for adults who want to discover how to build and maintain wealth and learn how to apply the wisdom in which to do it. In addition, this book is about learning how to get in a healthy money mindset, for people who need motivation to get their priorities in perspective. It also offers actionable techniques in an easy to digest format, to those who want to take control of their money, and it depicts how it can impact their live financially.

Furthermore, this personal finance book will educate and empower you to budget, save and get out of debt. It will also help you in handling challenges that come with money related decisions with confidence. Additionally, this book will assist you in understanding the increasing complexity of financial investments, in this era of innovation.

PART ONE:

CATCH THEM WHEN THEY ARE YOUNG

Chapter 1

The Basic Principles of Money

The theory of finance is being taught in schools, however, how to become rich and the wisdom of acquiring wealth are not taught in schools; it comes from the experience of practicing financial skills and the way we go about it in our everyday lives. Many parents do not discuss the issue of money with their children, and some adults were not taught on how to save, they learned the importance of saving money through trial and error; and that is because they must fend for themselves. That is the reason, so many kids grew up not knowing the importance of savings or know how to save. In this present time, children are now inquisitive about learning how to save money, they ask so many questions about money; and some talk about how rich they want to be in the future. However, most adults were not taught about the importance of saving money when they were young, so; how are they supposed to know how and what to teach their children about savings. Therefore, in this time and age, we must teach our children the importance of savings; and how beneficial it is for the future, but before we get into that, we first understand the principle of money.

The question to ask is: **What is the basic principle of money?**

In a simple explanation, the basic principle of money states that, when you spend less of every money or income you make; and you save the rest of the money, then, the savings become wealth. This principle will lead to increased wealth, because, by utilizing the savings in a wise way, putting it into small or big business ideas; it will cause the power of multiplication to increase the money tremendously, thereby making the person rich. Also, this principle or attitude will lead to a person having financial freedom to live comfortable in the present, and in the future.

Chapter 2

Some of the Techniques Parents Would Utilize to Teach Kids How to Save Money Responsibly

If you are a parent or parents with kids, or guardian to kids, it is very important to understand how to educate your kids about finance. To teach the kids the importance of savings from when they are little, and able to acknowledge what money is, and getting them to act on it; is one of the greatest ways of empowering the next generation. However, having a conversation with your kids about savings recurrently, is one of the most vital ways of teaching kids about money and the importance of savings. Please, make your kids know that establishing the principle of saving money from a young age is crucial, and it is a way of building a great secured financial future. Also, show the kids how to save money by practicing before them with a piggy bank, or a Jar with a lid on it for saving money. Moreover, the kids knowing that they can break the piggy bank, or take the whole money from the savings Jar when they are ready to deposit the money in the bank; to open a savings account, or buy whatever they wanted or invest the money on something important, is very crucial.

As I said earlier, some parents do not know how to discuss their financial situation with their kids, they think that if they discuss the financial situation with their kids, it will make their children look down on them; or think that they are not working hard enough to take care of them. Also, some parents do not know how to say "NO" to their kids whenever the kids ask them for something. Some parents will give their children money to buy expensive things, which the kids do not need, and some parents will choose to buy those expensive things themselves for their kids; and later struggle to feed their kids and pay bills. Their reason is that, they want their kids to be happy, even if it is for one day; and these parents have forgotten that the kids have the rest of their lives to be happy and not for one day out of their lives.

Please parents, do not get me wrong, your kids are meant to be happy; if possible, for the rest of their lives, but you must teach them how to do that morally and financially, or else they will be unhappy for the rest of their lives.

I will explain this statement I made to parents with a story about one of my friends and her kids.

A friend of mine who was a single mother of three kids as at when this happened, though, married now; was asking me if I know the type of gift she would give to her last child. Who was to become thirteen years, because she was running out of choice of gifts for the child, to make him happy. This her child was a boy, so, I asked her if the child has a savings account; and with the answer from her, I will know what to suggest to her. She said no, he doesn't have a savings account. I asked her why she has not yet opened a savings account for her son? She said that her son preferred to be given gifts most of the times, and that she did not open a savings account for the older kids, so; she had not thought of doing that for her last child. Also, she said that she doesn't know how to start the savings account discussion with her son, since her son already had things he wanted to buy with his birthday money. Though, expensive, but he wants to buy them because his friends are buying lots of expensive things. These were the answers my friend gave to me. So, I told her that I will like to have a chat with her son, and she accepted. She asked her son to come and see me the next day, telling him that I have something to give him for his thirteenth birthday. Her son was happy and he came to see me.

When my friend's son came to see me for the gift his mother told him I would give to him, I asked him some questions, and after that; I made my intention known to him.

The dialogue below illustrates some of the questions I asked him and the answers he gave to me:

Me: Son, I want to ask you some questions. Do you think that your mother is very rich, that she can buy anything you asked of her?

My friend's son: No, I don't know if my mom is rich or not, but she always buys me whatever I ask from her, like the things I requested from her for my birthday.

Me: How long have you been wishing, to buy these expensive items you wanted?

My friend's son: Since I saw my friends wearing them in school.

Me: What if your mother does not have enough money to give you, to buy those expensive clothes, shoes and other things you mentioned; since she has other responsibilities to take care of?

My friend's son: But it is my thirteenth birthday, she must buy those things for me or give me the money to buy them. I asked her for those things as gifts for my thirteenth birthday, and she promised that she will give me the money to buy them or buy them for me.

Me: How long will those gifts of expensive clothes, shoes and accessories last, for them to have wear and tear and you start wishing to have another one?

My friend's son: I don't know? All I know is that, I want to have them.

Me: Do you have a savings account?

My friend's son: No, what is a savings account? My mother has not told me anything about it.

Me: What of your father, has he discussed anything concerning you opening a savings account?

My friend's son: No, my father did not discuss anything about savings account with me, when I visited him.

On hearing that, I clearly explained to him that there is a difference between buying things that he needed and buying things because his friends have them. Also, I told him that, if he had known the importance of savings; and have a savings account, he would not be thinking of buying all those expensive things. He would have wanted to save some money and buy the things he needed with whatever remains of the money given to him anytime. Furthermore, I told him that whatever shoes, clothes or items he decides to buy for himself, that it is only him that will feel good about the clothes and shoes, not his friends. Buying expensive things or cheap things does not make him important nor feel satisfied for a long time, because the feelings of satisfaction would fade away after a little time. Satisfaction and happiness, come with whatever you have accomplish by yourself and not the expensive or cheap things you wear. I also told him that whenever he remembers that he has some money in his savings account, to buy whatever he needed at any time, he will be happy and would want to save more; that will give him the satisfaction he needed. While I was still talking, my friend's son started smiling, and I asked him why he was smiling. He said that, I was right in what

I said concerning the satisfaction he needed. Most times, after wearing those expensive clothes for some weeks or few months, he would feel like those expensive clothes, shoes and accessories are not important anymore, he will start feeling less satisfied with them and would want more other things. Then, he asked me, "What can I do to have the savings account, so that I can have the satisfaction you are speaking of"? I was happy with him because of the re-action, response and understanding he exhibited, so, I decided to give him the birthday gift I have for him. However, I gave him some amount of money for his birthday and asked him to use half of the money to open a savings account and use the remaining to buy whatever he wanted for himself. I also told him to start practicing that, beginning with his thirteenth birthday. All the money he would get from friends and family, he should keep the bigger part of it in the savings account and use the rest of the money for what he wants to buy for himself. Also, if he had nothing important to buy, then, he should put all the money given to him in his savings account.

After talking to him that day, he was very happy and I believed he learnt some great lessons from all I explained to him, and he will influence his friends with that; so, he went home. His mother saw me the next day and was very happy. S thanked me so much for the financial lesson which I taught her son and for the gift given to her son. So, I told her to teach her son more on how to differentiate between important things and less important things to buy; which is knowing the difference between needs and wants. So, with the experience I had with my friend and her son, I decided to talk to parents and guardians about it.

Therefore, there are some techniques or ways parents and guardians would utilize to teach their kids about the importance of savings and how to save. These techniques include:

i). Conversations about Money:

Starting a conversation about money and the importance of saving with your children is very vital, and it should not be a terrifying discussion, but should be a teaching and learning moment between parents and kids. Parents can start the discussion by emphasizing on the family values or ethics, also, discussing about working hard and spending responsibly. Parents should establish the system of allowance for their children and teach them how to save money through their allowances, and how they can save up for the things they want to buy. Also, parents should teach their children the meaning of needs and wants, and the difference of the two. Parents should ask their kids what they want to be in the future and how they want their future to look like. Furthermore, demonstrate how much their money can increase over the time if they start saving. The questions you ask your kids would help them learn to be optimistic, and have a positive relationship with money, which will assist them in thinking about long-term savings; and what type of investments they would make with their money in the future. Though, teaching your kids about how to save money might appear to be a difficult or hard task, but you can make the discussion to be fun all through the conversation. Also, you must encourage them to ask you some questions if they have one, it would help in their learning process.

ii). Buying a Piggy Bank or a Savings Jar for the Kids:

Buying a piggy bank for your kids or getting a savings jar, is one of the best ways of teaching kids how to save, while they practice how to do it. Also, it is vital to teach your kids that the aim for the piggy bank, or savings jar is to fill it with dollar notes and coins and using it to save for anything they need in the future. Parents should remind the kids that the more they save, the more the money increases for whatever they want to buy or use the money for. Also, whenever the savings jar or piggy bank is full of the saved money, always pour out the money and count the money with your kids; and write down the amount of money that was saved. Take your kids to the bank and open a savings account for them with the money. Let your kids understand how much money that was saved, and how the money would earn interests, if they leave the money there for a long time without taking it out. This would help the kids to understand the process of savings account in the bank, and the idea of interest as part of the growth of the money. Also, let the kids know that they can invest the money in a business, and gain interests as well.

I would let you know that my husband and I started with teaching my kids on how to save and the importance of savings, with these techniques and more.

iii). Lead the Kids by Examples:

Leading the kids by examples means that, after teaching your kids how to save money through savings jar or piggy bank, you should get your own savings jar which you put money recurrently; because children learn through example. Also, when you are out shopping with the kids, teach and show your kids how to discern or differentiate between different prices, and enlighten them on why purchasing one item is better than the other; because of its value and price.

iv). Create Timeline for the Kids:

Teachings are better when it is visualized, and the concepts of money can be very difficult to understand as kids. So, one of the techniques you can use to teach the kids about money, is by creating a timeline which your kids can visualize; and know when they reach the targeted goal. Assuming your kids receive $5 per week as allowance, and the target was to save for $50 or $100, in order to buy an important gift or item or use for something important. If we should use $50 as the targeted goal, then, what the parents must do is to get a book and a pen or marker. Draw a highlighted long line on one of the pages of the book and indicate '$0'on the beginning of the line and $50 at the end of the line. From the beginning of the line to the end of it, indicate some marks to show when they will reach to those points, before they get to their targeted goal; such as, 25%, 50%, 75%, and 100%. Also, parents should establish a reward system, where their kids would get a small reward whenever they get to any of the marked points, until they get to the targeted goal of $50. This would encourage them more on their savings goal. Also, always write down the amount of money that was saved any time you get to each of the marked points.

Furthermore, parents should inform their kids that it is important to create timeline and be disciplined about it, whenever they want to save up to buy something important or gift or to make an important payment anytime at the present or in the future.

To explain all these, I will tell you a story of what happened with my kids when they were little.

I have two kids and when they were little, that is 8 years and 6 years old. My husband and I started the conversation about money with them. We got them a piggy bank and taught them how to save with the allowance and other gift money they got from us and our family friends. I was so surprised about how the kids were asking us lots of questions, especially when we told them that they will be depositing their money in the bank when the piggy bank is filled up. The kids asked us why they will be depositing their money in the bank? What are the reasons and benefits of depositing their money in the bank? and what will be happening to the money in the future? My husband and I answered all their questions and more, telling them that they will be opening savings account with their saved money. Also, as little as the kids were then, we taught them about interest and compound interest and the difference of the two. Therefore, as parents you should always be prepared for financial conversation with your kids and the questions that come from the kids.

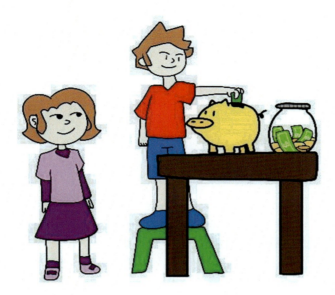

Figure 1.1

An example of teaching the kids on how to save. These kids are taking turns in putting their money in the Piggy Bank and the Savings Jar.

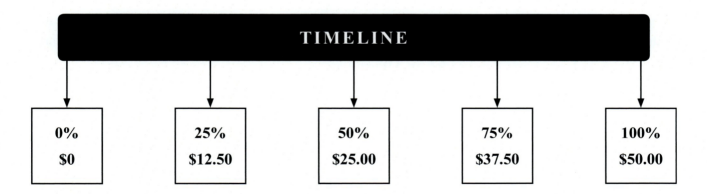

Figure 2.1

An example of the Timeline that should be used by parents to set a time limit for the kids on savings, for the targeted goal. The Timeline can have different amount depending on the targeted goal.

Chapter 3

Teaching Kids the Value of Money and Financial Management

Kids you can see that in the first chapter, I advised your parents on how to teach and motivate you on saving money and how important it is, to have savings account; but now, I will teach you how to get the money for your savings account, or whatever you want to buy with the saved money. Kids, there are so many approaches you can apply, to achieve success in the journey of money saving for a greater future. These approaches for getting money for your piggy bank, savings Jar and savings account are:

i). Request from Your Parents for an Allowance:

If you are a kid between the age of 7 and above, you should be old enough to be receiving allowance from your parents. Also, currently, kids younger than 7 years; are old enough to receive allowance from their parents. According to Experts report, it is vital for parents and guidance to start teaching their children about financial responsibility, as early as when they are in Kindergarten; because children who earn allowance, have better understanding of the value of hard work. So, as a 6 years or 7 years old kid, you can start by asking your parents for $5 a week; and as your age increases, they might increase your allowance. Also, if you are old enough to receive allowance from your parents, then; you must help in the house by doing some chores, this will be a confirmation to your parents that you understand how to be responsible.

ii). Recycling of Cans and Bottles:

As a kid, recycling cans and bottles, is a great way to put some little money into your pocket or let's say, your piggy bank. You can start by asking your parents for some big plastic bags for storing the empty cans and bottles, which you will be gathering and storing in the plastic bags. When the plastic bags are full, you must plead to your parents to assist you in selling them. With this, you will be saving the money gotten from the recycling, for your piggy bank and savings jar.

iii). Doing Extra Chores for Your Parents and Relatives in Exchange for a Little Payment:

You should know that kids do have chores which they do at home, to show their parents how responsible they are. So, at your free time, you can ask your parents, relatives or family friends; for extra chores to do for them in exchange for small payment. This will help you save some money for your piggy bank.

iv). Your Parents Opening a Savings Account for You or Buying You some Bonds as a Birthday Gift:

There are different types of child investment options parents can take up for their kids. As a kid, you can make a request from your parents, to open a savings account for you as a birthday gift. Also, you can ask your parents to buy the Series EE savings bond, issued by the government; for you as a birthday gift. This savings bond is an investment a child can own in his or her name, and it is an electronic EE savings bond, because U.S Treasury has stopped the selling of paper bonds since 2012. Furthermore, EE savings bonds can be purchased in any amount from $25 up to $10,000.

Figure 3.1

This picture is to show kids a little image of bank, where they would go to deposit money into their savings account.

Chapter 4

Financial Responsibilities and Management for Teenage Kids

i). Get a Part-Time Job:

As a teenage kid still in high school, getting a part-time job is a better way to make extra money for savings and gain a professional experience or knowledge. Depending on the law of the state you live in the United States, as from 14 years and above, a teenage kid can get a part-time job after school or during the school long holidays. However, in some states, it can be from 16 years old. So, you can ask your teachers and parents, on how you can create a resume; and how you can prepare for the job interview.

ii). Recycle Cans and Bottles or Selling Used and Unused Items:

As a teenage kid, you could recycle cans and bottles for cash. Also, you can sell some of your used and unused items. Such as: Used bicycles, Outdoor gears like Surfboards, Skateboards, Sports balls, Sleeping bags, Tents, etc. Depending on the area or location you live, if you ask for assistance of where you could sell them, your parents, guidance or other people would assist you on the information.

iii). Design a New Product:

As a teenage kid, if you are eager to do lots of work for long-term payments, you should write songs and sell it to some artists; you can also write a book. Furthermore, you can come up with creative ideas for a new product. Create the product and sell it, or you can sell the ideas of your creation. Also, you should ask your parents or guardians for assistance on how you can sell the product or the ideas. If you can create awareness with your product and so many people like it, then, it will make so much money for you. In addition, to the selling of your creative idea, if you could sell it to someone or a company, then, you will keep earning money or royalties from your work for a long-term.

iv). Make Money Online:

Listen, you teenage kids. There are several ways to make money online in this present time. One of them is starting a blog; with that, you can write about your teenage life, things kids do or any topic you are familiar with; that is interesting. When your blog site becomes prevalent or popular, and gains so much awareness then, you can sell advertising space; that will make lots of money for you. Another way of making money online is by creating videos of any interesting topics of your choice, to share with people online.

v). Start a Business of Your Own:

To start a business as teenage kid, it is vital that you are passionate about what you want to do, because you would want to enjoy the experience; and not to lose interest in the business and back out from it. Also, you must ask for the assistance of your parents or guardians to guide on it. Before starting the business, **firstly**, you should make a list of the types of business you will like to do and choose the best one you would be passionate about.

Secondly, write down the supplies, equipment and training you will need for the business. **Thirdly**, you should write down the reason you want to start the business. Such as, your financial goals for the business or any other thing you have in mind, which you want to accomplish by staring the business. Also, you must always have these goals in mind when running the business, because it will encourage and motivate you in the day-to-day activities of the business. Furthermore, to start a business of your own, you will need capital for it. So, you must write down the things you needed and the total amount it will require to start it. For capital for the business, get some money from your savings if you have one, and if you need financial assistance; then, you can ask your parents or guardians to invest in the business.

You must also learn and understand the importance of customer service, and how to explain or describe your product or service, communicating it in a good way to your customers; assuring them of the product or service value. If the business you chose to do needs a company structure, then, you should ask your parents or guardians to assist you with one. If they already have a Limited Liability

Company (LLC), they should add your company under it, but if they do not have one, then; they can establish an LLC company, and put your business under it, so that the business will be protected. Also, you should ask your parents or guardians to help you in filing tax return, especially when your earning would be higher than $400. As a child, you will not be able to file an income tax, but you will be paying for self-employment tax. **Lastly, you must understand that the business process should be enjoyable for you, and entrepreneurship should be a labor of happiness and bliss. In it, you must make mistakes and learn from your mistakes in the journey of the business, once you remember this all the time; then, you will succeed.**

In conclusion, if you are a teenage kid, whatever you decide to do in order to make money; the most important thing is for you to learn how to save, and have great savings for important things in life, and for bigger investments in the future.

*Therefore, it is vital for you to know that having the knowledge of investment, pays the best interests.

PART TWO:

NOW THAT WE ARE ADULT HOW DO WE BUILD AND INCREASE THE WEALTH?

Chapter 5

Having the Mindset to Create Wealth

In chapter one, I explained the basic principle of money in a very simple way by stating that, when you spend less of every income or money you make; and save the rest of the money. The whole money you have saved becomes wealth at that moment due to the value of money, which you will increase through making wise decisions and smart investments. If you are reading this book and you are a teenage kid who has just grown into adulthood, or you are an adult person who is searching, and want to know how you could have financial freedom; but do not know how to go about it. You must know that having the right mindset is the key and the beginning of your journey to financial freedom or creation of wealth.

However, you must be positive minded, be ready to make sacrifices and to take risks, then, you will be able to create immense wealth. Also, to have the mindset to create wealth or if you want to be wealthy, you must think like the wealthy. You must define or outline your financial goals and where you see yourself in few years to come, and ask yourself, how much money do you want to make in a year; five years, ten years or more in the future?

Nevertheless, to have the mindset to create wealth does not come easily. It means that a person must spend less, make wise decisions and investments, and must continue to look for ways to improve the financial position with low or little risk. Therefore, the requirements to develop the mindset to create wealth or to financial freedom include:

i). Being highly disciplined, upholding positive attitude, and having positive thoughts about wealth or richness.

ii). Knowing that a person is not defined by the person's present condition or what the person owns, but by the persons brilliant thoughts.

iii). Also, knowing that having business ideas is "Good", but the execution of these ideas created through your creative mind is the "Best"; and that will make the person successful.

However, in this era of innovation, it is very important to know that the best investment you can make is investing in yourself. The reason is that, by developing new skills, increasing or broadening your knowledge and understanding on different types of subjects, themes or topics; will increase the ability of you making more money. Investing in education, books, and programs, means that you are investing greatly into your future. Also, knowing that stocks can bust, housing market might collapse anytime, but, nothing or nobody will take away the knowledge and skills you have made as investments in yourself. These investments will turn you to be a better problem solver and being a better problem solver is the secret to being successful in business.

To explain this, I will tell you a story about investing in yourself through programs and seminars.

In the middle of year 2016, I was searching through the internet for some information, and I came across the information about a program; which is a seminar about Real Estate and Investments, that will be taking place in Sacramento, California. I was asked to register immediately, for one person or two, and so, I registered for two people. Though, there were different dates given for the seminar, but I picked the date convenient for my husband and myself. We went to the seminar to find out that they have lots of information to pass on to people about real estates and investments, and they requested that all the people present on that day should register for a three days seminar, which will be taking place in the next two weeks of that month. Also, we must make a payment to reserve a seat or seats for the three days seminar. One payment covers for one person or two people, that is, if you have a second person to bring for the three days seminar; but if not, the payment will be for you as a single person. Many people that made the payment on that seminar, tried to bring in another person, which should be value for their money. Well, My husband and I made one payment for both of us, and we attended the three days seminar which was in the evenings; from Friday through Sunday. I will be glad to say that the experience and knowledge we gained on the three days seminar was priceless, compared to the payment we made and the time we spent on the seminar. This led us (my husband and I) to register and establish a Limited Liability Company (LLC) for Real Estate and

Investments. Though, I later got an admission to study Chartered Finance Analysis and Investments, for my master's degree which helped in increasing my knowledge on investments and more on real estate. Well, the continuation of this story will be for another time.

However, what I was trying to explain through my story is that, my husband and I have been able to achieve lots of things due to the great knowledge acquired from the seminars we have been attending. So, this is an indication that investing in oneself through education, programs, seminars, books, etc., is a crucial step to being successful in life. Also, it depicts that one is taking the right steps towards developing the mindset to create wealth.

*Remember that Knowledge gained, will add no value to you, except when you put it into practice.

Chapter 6

The Power to Create Wealth

There is a saying which states that, "Knowledge is power". Therefore, gaining the knowledge to create wealth, is the power to create wealth. Also, we all are born with the power to create wealth. The power of the mind is very strong and effective, the mind must move before the money moves. Also, according to research, the strength or length of what human minds can do is limitless; and the mind have been empowered to create wealth and doing what we love to do or passionate about is the key foundation to funding our future.

Therefore, these are the key words to speak to yourself and the questions to ask yourself:

To build the Mindset to move to the next level, you should say to yourself: **"I have the ability to create wealth"** (speak this to yourself every day).

Then, ask yourself these questions:

- **What are the areas of my strength?**
- **What do I love doing or passionate about?**
- **How can I finance my abilities?**
- **What can I study or learn in my area of expertise?**

How to Establish the Power to Create Wealth:

Like I stated in chapter five, invest in yourself through paying for your education, programs, seminars, books, etc. Invest in anything that would add more knowledge and skills to your life. Also, discover what your area of expertise or talent is. What do you love doing or what are you passionate about? Do you love designing, sewing, painting, singing, writing, building, administration, etc.? The power of the mind is limitless, the only limits set, are the ones you set for yourself; if you declare in your mind that you will not limit yourself to success, then, you will be limitless.

Next, is to put action into your decision by pursuing your passion and positioning yourself for prosperity or for success. In doing that, you have taken the first step in establishing that you have the power to create wealth, all you need to do is put it into practice by turning your passion into profit. This is where investing in yourself on education, programs, etc. will be beneficial, because the knowledge and skills acquired from them will assist you in whatever passion you have chosen for yourself for business. Also, learn to enhance your skill periodically, to improve your knowledge or skills on your chosen field or to diversify yourself in other types of business. Though, personal growth and development is your choice, but you must also be eager to learn from those who are already where you want to be or who have made it by acquiring immense wealth successfully. Well, I will discuss this diversification of business in the next chapter.

Starting or Launching Your Business:

Another step to take, is putting your words into action, by starting or launching your chosen passion of business. If you are working, and you want to start your own business, one of the most crucial skills you will need to balance your daily job with running a side business; is a good time management skill. Also, if you are working on a daily job or not, time management is vital in the running of business. Understanding and learning to prioritize tasks will not be easy, but if you fail to prioritize your tasks, you might end up disappointing customers and vendors that need to work with you. Furthermore, prioritizing personal task is important so you can carve out enough time from your busy day, to devote to your business.

Capital for Starting Your Business:

Starting a business entails or requires money (capital), though, some business might not require much money. However, if you are buying an existing business, you will require to make a large payment for it. Depending on the type of business you have chosen to do, however, you must thoroughly do some research to know or calculate how much you would need to start up the business; and to maintain the business operations. In this innovative time, there are some basic important expenses that you must make for your business to be successful. These include:

- Having a website.
- Creating your business cards.
- Advertising your business.
- Having an accounting software for your business.
- Having a credit card processor account.
- Having a credit card/debit card machine for business transactions.
- Expenses for mailing supplies and postage.
- Having to rent a retail space for business (if applicable), that is, if you will not be selling your products or services online.
- How much it will cost you to obtain your products and store your products.

Furthermore, financing your business and its operations is very important, because starting a business without enough funds for its operations for at least 12 months or more; would cause the business to fail. Moreover, there are some business you can start with small amount of money by self-financing the business. While some other businesses might need large amount of money. If your business will need large amount of money to start it, then, you must create a good business plan; since you will require financing from other people or companies. When considering financing your business with large amount of money, apart from asking from your friends and family, and if you don't have cash in the retirement account; it entails that you will go for some companies or organizations that deal will assisting people with financing startup businesses, or those who want to grow their business. Therefore, these financing organizations are:

Small Business Administration (SBA) loans, Venture Capital (VC), Crowdfunding, Peer-to-Peer loans, National Business Incubator Association, and Angel Investors.

For the Angel Investors financing, there are some organizations that would put you in contact with Angel Investors, which include the individuals and the groups. So, these organizations are:

MicroVentures, Go4Funding, Investors' Cycle, Tech Coast Angels, Band of Angels, Golden Seeds LLC, Band of Angels, Hyde Park Angels, AngelList, Angel Capital Association, and Alliance of Angels.

However, you must know that putting together the financing to start a new business takes a serious planning and effort, unless you have enough money to finance your business. Also, an entrepreneur must weigh the advantages and disadvantages of the accessible or available funding options, to determine which sources of finance offer the utmost flexibility at the lowest cost.

Chapter 7

Strategic Ways to Increase Your Wealth

In this era of innovation, being creative gives one opportunity to try new ideas. It helps one to look at problems or situations from a new standpoint or perspective. Paying attention to your creative mind, and incorporate it more on whatever you are doing at the present, will assist you to set up strategic plans that will take you to the next level; which is from the point you are to the next point of increased success.

After graduating from the university, with my MSc in Chartered Financial Analyst & Investment, I came to understand the secret to building of wealth and the wisdom to continuous increased wealth. Which I would like to share with you:

Thus, a creative mind is an innovative mind, and to be a great innovator, you must be a good observer; and be ready to reverse lots of things, and change point of views to increase growth, either at your workplace or in your business. At your workplace, you must be a problem solver, be resourceful and discover some jobs that no one wants to do and do them. It will get your boss or manager to notice you and probably increase your wages or salary, better still, you can give the extra job a name and add it to your job at work; so, you then have two jobs at your workplace. With this, you can ask your boss or manager to increase your salary. If your boss or manger refuse to your request, then, you must look for another opportunity somewhere else; to see if you can combine two jobs and achieve your aim for increase of cash flow. The purpose for you to have this increase cash flow, is to invest some of the money somewhere resourceful, it is either on a business you will be active in; or in an investment which you will be passive in, while you are still working at your job. I will explain this later in this chapter.

However, if you own a business or a large company, you must have an innovative mind to set up strategic plans; that would take your small business or large company to the next level of higher growth. **Firstly,** you must ask yourself some questions, the answers to these questions will help you set up strategic plans; which will take you to the next level, from wherever point your small business or large company is standing. The questions are: **Why, Who, What, and How?**

i). Why: The answer to the question of why you should be creative and have innovative mind, is for your business to innovate and grow.

ii). Who: The answer to the question of who, can be explained in two ways, which are:

1). If you own a small business in this innovative time, for your business to get to the next level, it is mandatory that you hire or employ someone that has more creative mind; and is more talented or knows more than you, in your line of business. Also, depending on how much your budget is, you may hire at least one or more creative and talented people; who will help you take your business to the next level. Furthermore, apart from the salary you will pay to them, you may offer them little percentage of shares or partnership in your business; for them not to look elsewhere. This will motivate them to work very hard for the business to grow to a higher level, and for every one of you to benefit from it.

2). If you own a large company, you should employ or hire talented people such as: Accountants, Financial Analysts, Human Resources, talented people with different knowledge about different things, into the organization; and create a department for them to be creative. They will be cultural contributors to the organization, rather than being cultural fit for the organization. This group of people that are known as cultural contributors, will continue to concentrate or focus on creating innovative ideas that will take the organization to the next level, thereby increasing its growth to a higher level.

iii). What: The answer to the question of what is: For the organization to measure the results of the output of its innovative investments, to know if it is turning into something useful or beneficial to the organization. Businesses or organizations must learn to be highly innovative to be able to: **Create, Manage, Extend and Adapt to innovation**. By the development of customer value, from the solutions that meet fresh needs, implicit or undefined needs, or already existing needs; in the exceptional or unique methods.

The explanation to this statement is:

To Create: Is for an organization or business to innovatively create products or services in a ground-breaking technique.

To Manage: Is for an organization to make a change on an existing product or service in an innovative way, by redesigning it for an improved use, and maintaining the new design. The product will be efficient for the same users but would have more types of offering to the consumers.

To Extend: Is for an organization to innovatively take an existing product and change or extend its use for additional or more value for the users.

To Adapt: Is for an organization to adapt to innovation, by gradually developing or transforming a product from a simple form to a complex one which would be of great value to the consumers.

However, whichever choice of innovative investments is utilized by an organization, be it one, two or all of them, it is crucial for it to be beneficial to the organization in terms of measuring the outcome.

iv). How: The answer to the question of how, is for an organization to measure the results of innovative investments, which will lead it to build innovatively and will lead to learning more of the innovative techniques. Also, for the organization to keep repeating this procedure.

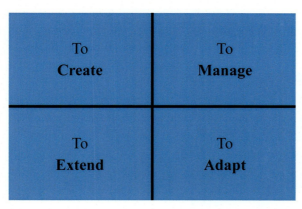

Figure 4.1

An example of an Innovation Metric.

Secondly, you will recall that I talked about being passive in other businesses or investments earlier in this chapter, for the purpose of additional cash flows. So, it is time to discuss about passive investments. If you have a 9 – 5 job or you have a business, multiple investments are some of the channels you can utilize in gaining additional cash flows. Index funds offer you an access to invest in the stock market which is entirely passive, and if you invest in an index fund such as S&P 500 Index, it means that you are investing in the universal or general market, with less worries or anxiety about diversifying your portfolio; picking investments, and buying and selling stocks of different companies, because the fund of your portfolio will manage all the activities. Also, there are some index funds arranged for every market segment, such as: Precious Metal, Energy, Banking, Emerging Markets, etc. So, you will only select and pay for the market sectors you would like to partake in, and the fund of your portfolio will manage your selections for you.

Furthermore, Diversification is the key to mitigating risks on investments, and by diversifying your portfolio as an investor; you are guiding against risks and protecting your investments against market volatility.

However, one of the ways you can guide against risk is by investing on index funds, and in other businesses; making you a passive business owner in those businesses and relieving you of the stress of managing business operations. Also, to purchase or invest on index funds, you should search for investment companies, brokerage or banks that deals with index funds, especially the ones that charge low fees on their account. Though, there are some risks involve with index funds but, they might be very low, and one of the advantages is that your money will be managed for you in a better way.

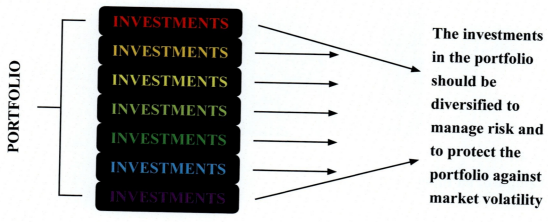

Figure 5.1

Chapter 8

How to Continuously Increase and Maintain Your Wealth in this Era of Innovation

Before I go on to discuss this topic, I would like you to cast your mind back to the 2008 financial crisis, which was the worst economic disaster since the Great Depression of 1929; and it occurred in spite of the federal reserve and Treasury Department efforts to prevent it. However, it is only change that is constant, but all other things can change at any time. No one is praying or wishing for economic crisis or inflation, but it might happen again, and nobody knows when. Do not be caught unawares when it happens again. So, creating strategic plans on how to build and maintain your wealth, should be your utmost priority. Today is the earliest time you should start building wealth and set-up strategic plans, on how to continuously increase your wealth, for a continuous better life for you and your family.

Let me tell you something. Before I graduated from my master's degree program in finance, I was able to attend a seminar on "The Importance of Building Wealth"; one of the speakers asked the audience this question, "Who amongst you all wants to know the techniques of continuously increasing wealth?" Do you know that everybody in the audience raised their hands? Yes, everybody that came to that seminar raised their hands. This is to show that many people are unceasingly searching for techniques or ideas on how to increase their wealth or income.

However, in this innovative era; there are some knowledge or ideas which you would apply that would assist you in your quest or pursuit. Nevertheless, there are lots of solutions and ideas on how to increase your wealth, but I will be discussing some major solutions and ideas in this chapter, and they are:

1). Reducing Your Debts and Expenses and Paying Off Your Mortgage:

One of the most important things you should do when you want to increase your wealth, is to create strategies to reduce your debts and expenses, because the less money you spend; the more money you would accumulate in net worth or in wealth. Have a look at your current expenses, to know if there are some things or expenses you can cut back.

You should know that there are differences between needs and wants. Your needs are some of the things you must have for you to live or be alive, while your wants are the things you wish to have for you to add comfort to your live.

Therefore, your needs signify necessities, whereas your wants depict your desires. So, you should strategize on how to cut back on the expenses on your wants, and in reducing your debt. Furthermore, avoid credit card debt. Having multiple credit cards debt, are what lead to increased expenses. If you must have a credit card, then, you should go for the ones that have low APR and the ones that give cash back ranging from 1% to 5%, this will give you the chance to earn some passive income indirectly, because with the reward on cashback and points, you can pay for things which is to your advantage.

Another way to reduce your expenses or debts is to pay off your mortgage. Mortgage payment is one of the major debts which you may have because of the accumulating interests on the mortgage. You should check whether you can pay off your mortgage if you have the money, so that you can get a larger amount of debt off your book. Also, making the mortgage payments bi-weekly, is a better way to quicken or fast-track paying off your mortgage.

2). Diversifying your Cash flow streams:

In wealth building or to continuously increasing your wealth, having multiple streams of income is the key factor. Whatever your job or profession is, including the highly paid professionals, having multiple cash flow streams is the most efficient way of building wealth. As a highly paid professional, for example: A medical doctor, having a single cash flow stream, which is from your daily job is good;

but in this innovative era, it is important to be mindful of the past economic crisis and plan strategically towards being prepared whenever it occurs, and as well, working towards accelerating your growth for financial freedom. Therefore:

The best way to build wealth is to create multiple cash flow streams through your active income, and the more you make money through your cash flow streams, the more you should re-invest the money into creating more cash flow streams. With that, you will continuously increase and maintain your wealth, unless you make a mistake on the line. That is the reason you must always upgrade your knowledge periodically on wealth creation, to mitigate risks that come on the way with creating wealth.

Furthermore, you must also have a special savings account for emergencies. This account will help to solve any problems that comes up in the family, and for leisure or holiday trips for you and your family. This emergency fund will enable you to build on your cash flow streams without intercepting or disrupting your wealth creation.

However, some of the diversified cash flow streams you can create for your wealth building are: Business Income (Cash Stream), Interest Income (Cash Stream), Capital Gains (Cash Stream), and Royalties/Licensing (Cash Stream).

You can have as many as you can be able to create and manage them efficiently. I will explain more on the types of cash flow streams, below in this chapter.

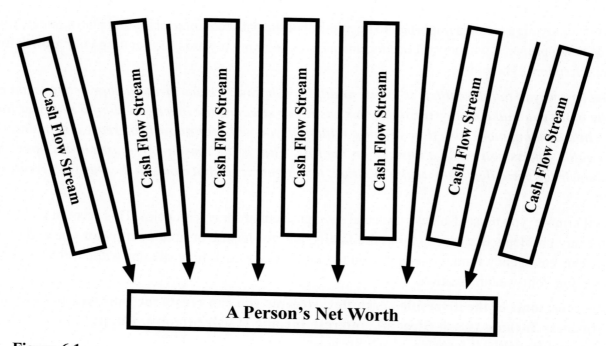

Figure 6.1

An image of the cash Flow Streams driving and channeling towards a person's net worth.

3). Set-up websites for selling Products or Services:

Setting up a website for selling products or services is classified under Business Income (Cash Flow Stream). These products or services may be created and manufactured by you or they can be products and services from other people. The most important factors here are, that you are knowledgeable about the products and services in order to sell them; and that it is generating revenues. However, if you can be able to ship the products from the manufacturers to the customers without much work on it, that would be better; because it is one of your passive income.

4). Investing in Real Estate Investment Trusts (REITs):

Investing in Real estate Investment Trusts (REITs), is classified under the Business Income (Cash Flow Stream). This is a way of being a passive landlord, and you can start this investment with small amount of money, instead of the big amount of money used in buying a house or apartment. Real Estate Investment Trusts (REITs) is like a mutual fund that is holding different real estate projects and the fund is managed by professionals, which means that you would not be getting involve in managing the fund. One of the great advantages of someone investing in REITs is that, they will pay you higher dividends that bonds, stocks and bank investments. Also, one can sell the interest on a REITs whenever the person wants to do so, and that makes it very liquid, because it is better than owning real estate.

However, you can also invest in Real Estate property, if you have large amount of money to invest in business. Though, this may be under the segment of semi-passive income, it is semi-passive because there are some professional property managers, that can manage the property for you for some percentage of the monthly rent; such as 10% or a little bit more, so with the professional managers, you would be passive in your investment, however, it will cost you some money which will affect your cash flow with a little amount.

Furthermore, in rental properties, buying smart is the only technique to be successful in real estate; because it is not every property an investor buys would deliver good return. So, learning how to evaluate a potential property is very crucial to be successful in real estate. Also, one the advantages of investing in real estate is the loan repayment. Let's say that you took out a loan to purchase some rental properties and each month, the tenants are paying off some parts of the loan. When the mortgage on the rental properties are paid off by the tenants, all other monthly payments by the tenants would be your cash flow, which would highly increase at that period. Then, the cash flow would become a passive income for you and create a better life for you and your family.

5). Open an Account with a Better Bank:

When you open a savings account with a better bank that pays higher interest rate, which is having a high yield savings account, you would be earning some couple of hundreds of dollars a year. This is a good start for earning revenue, because the more money you would deposit the more your money would grow. This is classified under the Interest Income (Cash flow Stream). Also, this is one of the easiest ways to enhance your income and it is a passive income too. In addition, your money would be insured under FDIC, so that you will not lose the money. Though, the general average savings account interest is at 0.09% at present, however; you can search for banks that pays a better interest or higher interest rate on savings, open a savings account with them and start earning some money.

Figure 7.1

Always search for innovative banks with high interests on savings account. It is one of the ways to increase revenue in wealth creation.

6). Purchase High Dividend Stocks:

Purchasing high dividend stocks is classified under Dividend Income (Cash Stream). Dividend income is the money that is distributed amongst shareholders, for owning shares in a company. However, with high dividend stocks, there is potential for capital appreciation. So, with that the owner can earn passive income from two sources, which are: From dividend and capital gains. Also, have it in mind that you will need to open a brokerage account, to buy the high dividend stocks.

7). Become a Business Passive Partner:

Becoming a business passive partner is classified under the Business Income (Cash Stream). For this type of cash stream, you must search for any successful business that the owner or owners need capital for expansion. With that, you can become an angel investor to the business by offering or providing the required capital to the business. In this aspect, you will also be taking an equity position in the business as a partner but will be a passive one; earning some profits from it, while the daily operations of the business will be taken care of by the owner or owners.

Becoming a passive business partner, is one of the key techniques of how to build and continuously increase your wealth, while maintaining whatever job or business you are doing; and become passive partner or owner of so many successful businesses.

In conclusion, building and increasing wealth is not about wishing for it alone, but by utilizing strategic plans which are designed to address all the areas of your financial quest. Also, by putting your wishful thinking into action, you can set yourself firmly on the part to a higher financial greatness.

*Remember that in everything we do, making mistakes and learning from the mistakes, comes great success.

*So, you must say to yourself right now, "Do not get ready, Get Started."

Other resources

*Below is an Important Message to Parents and Guardians With Kids Concerning this Book of Magical Stories.

Magical Stories for the Special Princes and Princesses in Our Lives

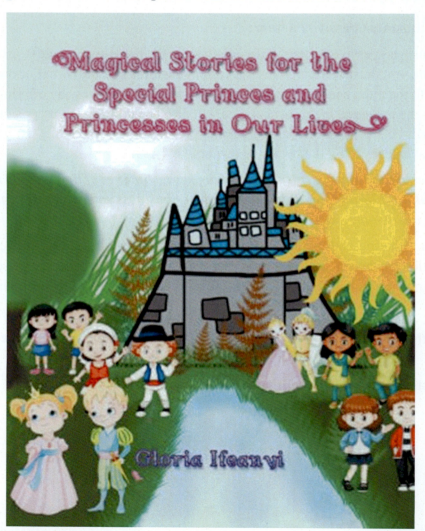

This book of fictional magical stories was written for kids who love reading and are excited about magic, and for parents who loved their kids and believed that their children are the special princes and princesses in their lives. Magical stories can be a way to get kids who are disinclined to reading, to enjoy reading books.

Are you trying to get your students more involved as readers? Maybe as a teacher, you are beginning a unit in class on magic or fantasy, or possibly, you have just perceived that your kids are really interested in magic; and you want to take advantage of this fascination. Whichever is your motivation, it can be helpful to have a set of engaging stories that you can use to sustain students' interest in magic.

The lessons from these stories will help grow kids' imaginations and their love for reading, while learning about: Courage, obedience, honesty, kindness, friendship, respect and love for one another.

Furthermore, in each of the story in this book, there are some moral lessons to learn, please endeavor that the kids take note of this lessons and talk about them, because it will help in building their personal characters.

Get Your Copy Now!!!

www.Xlibris.com

www.Amazon.com

www.barnesandnoble.com

Printed in the United States
By Bookmasters